**W9-BHR-320**

WITHDRAWN

ROCKFORD PUBLIC LIBRARY

Rockford, Illinois

www.rockfordpubliclibrary.org

815-965-9511

AREA 51

BY NADIA HIGGINS

EPIC

BELLWETHER MEDIA · MINNEAPOLIS, MN

EPIC BOOKS are no ordinary books. They burst with intense action, high-speed heroics, and shadows of the unknown. Are you ready for an Epic adventure?

This edition first published in 2014 by Bellwether Media, Inc.

No part of this publication may be reproduced in whole or in part without written permission of the publisher. For information regarding permission, write to Bellwether Media, Inc., Attention: Permissions Department, 5357 Penn Avenue South, Minneapolis, MN 55419.

Library of Congress Cataloging-in-Publication Data

Higgins, Nadia.
  Area 51 / by Nadia Higgins.
    pages cm. – (Epic. Unexplained Mysteries)
  Summary: "Engaging images accompany information about Area 51. The combination of high-interest subject matter and light text is intended for students in grades 2 through 7"– Provided by publisher.
  Audience: Ages 7-12.
  Includes bibliographical references and index.
  ISBN 978-1-62617-101-5 (hardcover : alk. paper)
  1. Area 51 (Nev.)–Juvenile literature. 2. Air bases–Nevada–Juvenile literature. 3. Research aircraft–United States–Juvenile literature. 4. Unidentified flying objects–Juvenile literature. I. Title.
  UG634.5.A74H54 2014
  358.4'170979314–dc23
                        2013036465

Designed by Jon Eppard.

Printed in the United States of America, North Mankato, MN.

TABLE OF CONTENTS

KEEP OUT!

A car drives down State Route 375 past Rachel, Nevada. The driver watches the sky for **UFOs**. After all, he is on the **Extraterrestrial** Highway!

Soon the driver takes a right onto Groom Lake Road. A sign warns about a **restricted area** called Area 51. Military guards are watching him. He quickly turns the car around.

WARNING
MILITARY INSTALLATION

IT IS UNLAWFUL TO ENTER THIS INSTALLATION WITHOUT THE WRITTEN PERMISSION OF THE INSTALLATION COMMANDER.

INSTALLATION COMMANDER
AUTHORITY: Internal Security Act, 50 U.S.C. 797
PUNISHMENT: Up to one year imprisonment and $5,000. fine.

YOU SHALL NOT PASS

Sensors and helicopters also help guard Area 51. People who enter can go to jail!

TOP-SECRET BASE

Area 51 is an Air Force base in the Nevada desert. The United States government built the base in 1955. They needed a **remote** place to test **spy planes**.

NEVADA

AREA 51

YOU NAME IT

Area 51 has many other names. It is also called Paradise Ranch, Dreamland, and Groom Lake.

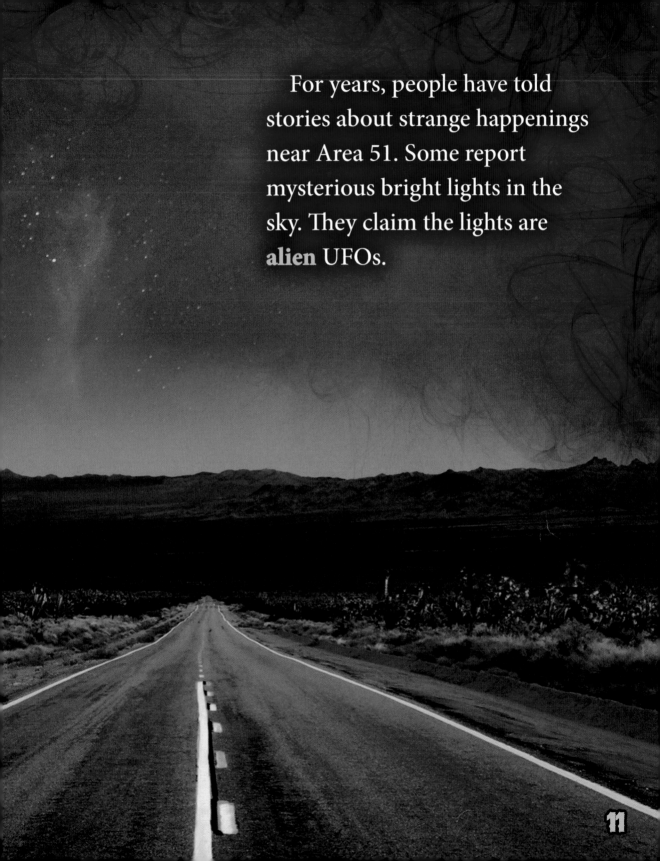

For years, people have told stories about strange happenings near Area 51. Some report mysterious bright lights in the sky. They claim the lights are **alien** UFOs.

In 1989, a scientist named Bob Lazar shocked the world. He said he studied alien spaceships near Area 51. Many people thought his story was a **hoax**.

UFO ALERT?

Some people believe Lazar. They think Area 51 is home to crashed UFOs. A few even believe aliens live on the base.

Believers claim scientists study the alien technology. The government uses their research to develop new aircraft.

Skeptics say aliens have nothing to do with Area 51. They argue it is kept secret to protect military technology.

AIRCRAFT TESTED AT AREA 51

Aircraft: U-2 spy plane
Special Feature: Can fly too high for enemies to attack it

Aircraft: A-12
Special Feature: Could fly higher than any other airplane

Aircraft: SR-71 Blackbird
Special Feature: Could fly up to 2,200 miles (3,540 kilometers) per hour

Aircraft: F-117 Nighthawk
Special Feature: Could not be seen by enemy planes because of a special coating

Aircraft: MQ-1 Predator
Special Feature: Can spy and attack with no pilot, crew, or windows

F-117 Nighthawk

We may never know the secrets hidden within Area 51. The few people with information must keep quiet. Is the military working with advanced

GLOSSARY

alien—a being from another planet

extraterrestrial—an alien being

hoax—an attempt to trick people into believing something

remote—far away from where a lot of people live

restricted area—an area where only certain people are allowed to be

skeptics—people who doubt the truth of something

spy planes—military planes that spy on enemies to gather information

UFOs—mysterious objects found in the sky; UFO stands for "unidentified flying object."

TO LEARN MORE

At the Library

McClellan, Ray. *Alien Abductions*. Minneapolis, Minn.: Bellwether Media, 2014.

Perish, Patrick. *Are UFOs Real?* Mankato, Minn.: Amicus, 2014.

Shea, Therese. *Spy Planes*. New York, N.Y.: Gareth Stevens Pub., 2013.

On the Web

Learning more about Area 51 is as easy as 1, 2, 3.

1. Go to www.factsurfer.com.

2. Enter "Area 51" into the search box.

3. Click the "Surf" button and you will see a list of related Web sites.

With factsurfer.com, finding more information is just a click away.

INDEX

The images in this book are reproduced through the courtesy of: Ralf Juergen Kraft/ photoBeard, front cover (composite), pp. 14-15 (composite); emattil/ Dudarev Mikhail, pp. 4-5 (composite); Department of Defense, pp. 6, 21; Maxim Petrichuk, p. 7 (top); SipaPhoto, p. 7 (bottom); Juan Martinez, pp. 8-9; David M. Schrader/ Andrea Crisante, pp. 10-11 (composite); tawan, p. 12 (top); Minerva Studio/ Chromatika Multimedia snc, pp. 12-13 (composite); Dmitry Kalinovsky, pp. 16-17; Nicholas/ Getty Images, pp. 18-19.